The Integrity of God's Word for a Greater Destiny

A Courtship & Marriage Discipline

Manual for Successful Daily Living

By Janet Adenusi

DEDICATION

This book is dedicated to Almighty God, the creator of the universe, the author and the finisher of our faith. The God who draws water with a basket to put the devil to shame, because only God is **SUPERNATURAL**.

He said to me, "This is the word of the Lord to Zerubbabel: Not by might, nor by power, but by my spirit, says the Lord of hosts.
- Zechariah 4:6, NIV

This book is orchestrated by God for Courtship and Marriage Discipline for a greater destiny. This refers to a commitment to principles and behaviors that build a strong, lasting courtship and marriage on the foundation of God, which fosters mutual respect, effective communication, and shared values for a sustainable home. The key disciplines set out by God in a Godly relationship include open communication, forgiveness, mutual submission, spiritual growth, faithfulness, and the intentional growth into a good, ready spouse, couples, and marriages. This approach emphasizes self-control and deliberate action to create a harmonious union and a healthy foundation for a lifelong covenant marriage that is embedded in a HOLY BODY OF CHRIST (non-defilement of the body). Having understood that the principles of God are also paramount to nurture and birth the mandate and vision of God, as a chosen generation who believes and feeds on nothing but THE WORD OF GOD. To all who are depressed, bound, limited, discouraged, confused, oppressed, and ready to end it all, who have found no meaning to the purpose of their creation on earth? I want you to know that you are born for a purpose, to occupy a position. What kind of purpose is your living and position today?

There is no one on earth who is challenge-free, so I want you to know that you are not alone... God will destroy every shackles of hell in your life, and home in Jesus Name.

CONTENTS

ACKNOWLEDGEMENT

To God be the Glory for his mighty hand upon me and my family, my Heavenly   Father, the one who orchestrated my birth to this world for a purpose. The great author of wisdom and understanding who has brought me far in his work and life, the creator of the universe who has the world in his palm, He has always been my strength and pillar. My father in heaven: I Love You So Much. To my parents, they were chosen by God as the caretakers of my birth. My life has been a testimony, having come from this strict Christian family. My parents were so committed to the things of God and community work   ; this gave me a good head start and opportunity to observe, to assist in wiping the tears of many who are attacked by the shackles of hell, through their engagement with community and gospel work. This book forms   part of the work embarked on to do in this God Ordained Glowing Generation, whereby God will be releasing bound destinies, destroying the stronghold of demons, and birthing his glory upon so many souls. Imparting the world with the rising power of God over all who are passionate about victory. Everyone I have met and those around me, you have been a blessing in one way or the other   . I therefore acknowledge you all, for everything created by God was created for a purpose. I appreciate you all. To my best friend of life, my ribs and my bones, my helpmate and anointed man of God   , Kenny Adenusi, I am proud of you for all your support, prayers, and contributions to this book. You are indeed my God given destiny helper till eternity. The gifts of our union, our daughters and sons: Jesus is Mine, Enjoy the goodness of God, Favour, Divine,

Marvel, and Covenant Adenusi, you all are forever blessed till eternity in the name of God. Keep the fire of God burning   . Thank you for being a blessing to your generation through the gospel of God. Watching you all grow in spiritual attainment is a phenomenon: Thank you, Jesus! !! !!!

To my spiritual parents, I am eternally grateful to God for belonging to a glowing generation family and of the Issachar family. You have been instrumental in my spiritual journey. I express my gratitude to God for your Heavenly wisdom, guidance, and prayers which contributed to my spiritual expansion and flourishing. Thank you. I love you and God bless you abundantly! !! !!!

INTRODUCTION

This book is dedicated to God ; it is designed by God to destroy the yoke of satanic deposits in courtship and marriages. To release the Godly blissful union and home that God has designed from the onset of creation. God showed me the turmoil and the issues that our generation goes through today in their relationship and marriages, in the hands of the devil ; in the beginning, it wasn't so.

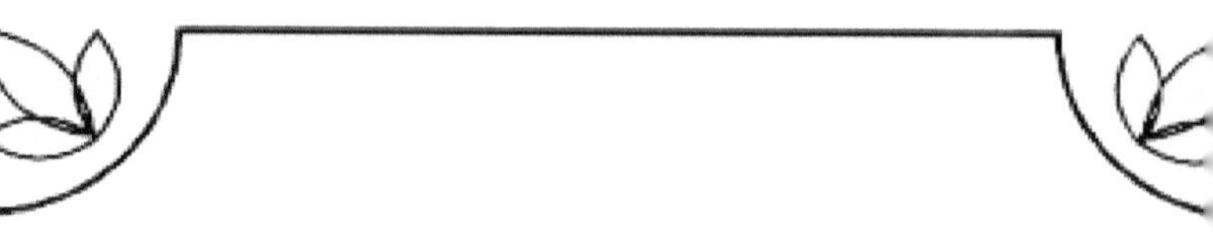

Jesus replied, "Moses permitted you to divorce your wives because your hearts were hard. But it was not this way from the beginning."

Matthew 19:8, NIV

"Therefore a man shall leave his father and his mother and hold fast to his wife, and they shall become one flesh."

Genesis 2:24, NIV

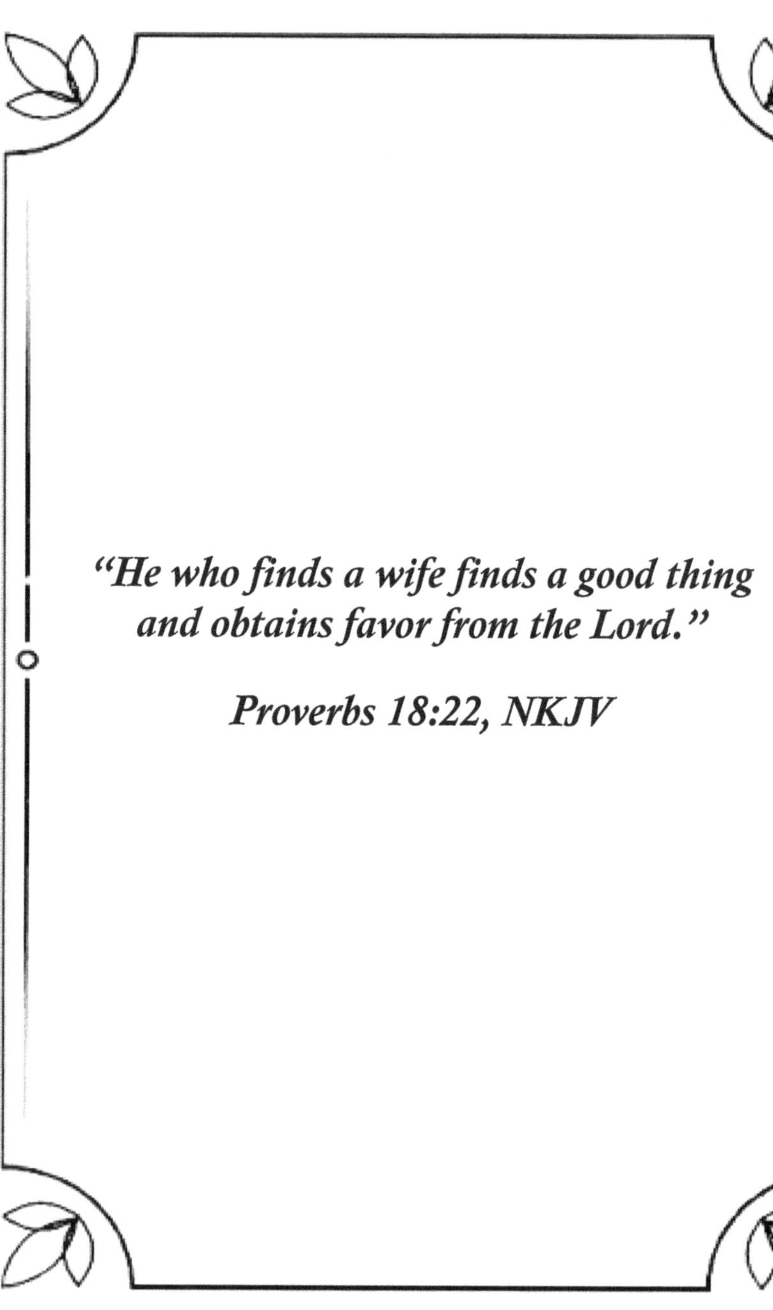

"He who finds a wife finds a good thing and obtains favor from the Lord."

Proverbs 18:22, NKJV

I was blessed by God to have made positive impacts   on people's relationships and marriages. Although in previous book/s, magazines, counselling sessions, conferences and seminars, I was privileged by God to speak and write on how to make a good home as a woman. Tremendous testimony has been born through these channels. I have had people asking for more in-depth books on the areas   where they are mostly challenged, which is not really talked about, and this solidifies the revelations God showed me, seeing people bound and destroyed by the devil. Reading this book, God wants to set you free and help you reach your goal in life with His integrity in His words for your greater destiny.

CHAPTER ONE

What is God's Word of Integrity for a Greater Destiny

The integrity of God's Word for a greater destiny simply means the assertion of God's words in the Bible is a pure, trustworthy, and powerful source of truth that can transform a person's life, granting them Godly wisdom, freedom, and a divinely intended path for a prosperous destiny. God's word emphasizes integrity in courtship and marriage through His principles.

This kind of integrity I am talking about stems from what is called God's own character, because our God is truthful and faithful to His promises,

God's Word is ever dependable and reliable, guiding for faith and conduct that is ultimately received, applied, and leads to an ever purposeful and fulfilling life.

Many homes are destroyed, marriages experienced or experiencing divorce, the world is occupied with escalating numbers of single mothers/ fathers. Spouses are hurting because there are cracks in their marriages as a result of not understanding the integrity of God's word for every believer to live a fulfilling life for a greater destiny. This has forced numerous individuals to navigate life without a partner and to rebuild their lives, most times appearing impossible. These had resulted in emotional toll, financial burden, crisis, destructive behaviors, substance abuse, divorce, single parents and polygamous homes.

A Godly courtship and marriage discipline is the set of principles and behaviors guiding a committed relationship, that is focusing on self-control, mutual respect, and commitment to build a strong, lasting partnership in their courtship and marriage.

To understand the concept of God's Word of Integrity for a Greater Destiny in courtship and marriage, let's look at what the Bible says:

> *"So is my word that goes out from my mouth: It will not return to me empty, but will accomplish what I desire and achieve the purpose for which I sent it"*.
>
> **- Isaiah 55:11, NIV**

Many believers have drifted away from the word of God and basically live on the earthly word. For example, you see and hear the wisdom of man (earthly wisdom) everywhere, and with a great decline in Godly wisdom.

Heavenly (Godly) wisdom is the wisdom of God that God gives to his children: this kind of wisdom is given to the FOOLISH: those that are MEEK, those who possess this appear to be very quiet because they have to give God the audience to be audible, they are occupied with the things of God because they do not walk in their own wisdom (human/ earthly wisdom) but on GOD'S WILL. They decrease their volume so that God can increase His volume.

For the foolishness of God is wiser than human wisdom, and the weakness of God is stronger than human strength.

- 1 Corinthians 1:25, KJV

Godly integrity is a deeper, faith-based expression of this virtue, which involves aligning with God and living your entire life with God. This is driven by a desire to honor God and reflect His character. Years back, I was officiating a marriage ceremony, and the message God gave to me was titled: Behind Closed Doors. During my sermon, I discovered the message was hitting the congregation   ; it was deep, resonant, and impactful, eliciting strong spiritual and emotional responses from the congregation   . This led to actions like renewed faith, praise, a desire to live accordingly, and salvation being restored. You can't run a relationship or home on earthly wisdom   ; it would crack, and God will be absent from it.

Therefore,

To everyone reading this book today, as singles or couples, I pray for patience, guidance, and Godly wisdom for you in Jesus Name. God's divine plan for you will unfold, leading to fulfillment and a loving relationship in a happy and Godly marriage in Jesus Name.

God will give you an unshakeable bond that will produce a strong Godly family and remain faithful to one another, grow old together in good health, and health and vitality in Jesus Name.

"God is not human, that he should lie, not a human being, that he should change his mind. Has he said it and will he not do it? Has he spoken and will he not fulfill it?"

- Numbers 23:19, NIV

As you read this book, I pray for God's wisdom to give you understanding and the light of God to shine in your lives, relationships, marriages, and home in Jesus Name. Amen!

So they rose early in the morning and went out into the Wilderness of Tekoa; and as they went out, Jehoshaphat stood and said, "Hear me, O Judah and you inhabitants of Jerusalem: Believe in the LORD your God, and you shall be established; believe His prophets, and you shall prosper."

- 2 Chronicles 20:20, NKJV

CHAPTER TWO

What are the types of God's Integrity that He expects from us for a greater destiny in courtship & marriage?

How do you   understand the Integrity of God's Word~

By His Truth and Purity:

God's Word is very pure and the truth itself, providing a perfect and reliable foundation.

The purity part entails making sure that you keep yourself holy: To keep your body holy, free from adultery/ fornication, this involves recognizing your body as a sacred temple of the Holy Spirit, as described in the book of **1 Corinthians 6:18-20, NKJV.**

This requires actively fleeing sexual immorality and cultivating purity of thought through biblical understanding, prayer, and avoiding compromising situations to honor God with your body and spirit.

Testimony:

To the Glory of God, and please listen, I am not saying this to disparage anyone reading this book who wasn't able to preserve his/her body for Christ. It is to encourage you and bring clarity to the integrity of God's word on courtship and marriage.

I met my better half as a virgin, and I have never strayed away or compromised with my body because it is a covenant with God. This is pure God's faithfulness.

Many people will say, Rev Janet, I was tempted, I just couldn't resist the temptation, I couldn't preserve my body. Beloved, I know it takes the grace of God to make your body holy. Now, let's go deep on how to sustain your body for God, not defiling your body.

You must understand that to sustain your body for God means to care for your physical and mental well-being as a way to honor God, recognizing your body as a temple of the Holy Spirit. Why do I mention mental health   well-being   ? It is because defiling your body starts from the lust of the eyes   ? Yes, you must understand that your eyes are directly connected to your brain by what is called   the optic nerve, which acts as a cable, that is transmitting electrical signals from the retina to your brain. Now, the retina converts light into these signals, and your brain begins to process them to form the images you see and these images then enable you to perceive colors, shapes, and movement and in return triggers you to act.

Lustful looking is a temptation that leads believers to stray away from God's will, and therefore, you are encouraged to guard your eyes and redirect your focus to spiritual matters, or identify distraction techniques that are taught in counselling during such periods to resist temptation.

How do you keep your body holy and in purity?

By Fleeing from Sexual Immorality:

The Bible made us understand that we must "flee from fornication" and all forms of sexual immorality, including adultery. All other sins a person commits are outside the body, but whoever sins sexually, sins against their own body~

- 1 Corinthians 6: 18, NIV

What do you do? As singles avoid staying alone with your   fiancée in places during courtship until you are married due to vulnerability of the flesh, remember when you follow the desires of a sinful nature, the results are very clear:

sexual immorality, impurity, lustful pleasures, are all defilements of the body ~

- Galatians 5:19, KJV

How does this work? A typical Life Example.

During courtship with my better half, we would stay away from places that are secretful, and always chat at open places where my families are present. During meetings, we only discuss progress in our lives and what our future ambitions are. He will advise me on steps to take on my career goals and I will lead mostly on the spiritual aspect, which is praying together.

**Make your courtship an open relationship   .
How?**

During my courtship, my parents were very involved, I was very open about it, nothing to hide and this was my making, through the wisdom of God. I discussed all our discussions and meetings with my parents, handing over anything he buys or gives to me,   including cards, letters, and many more. My parents are in control and advise me on how to respond to his letters while alerting my   fiancée that I presented his gift to my family, and it was approved that I can accept it. This enhanced a high degree of respect for me. I remembered my better-half telling me one day, I will never defile your body, I will only touch your body until I marry you.

He told me my sibling and my parents told him I am a virgin and he has promised everyone he will never mess me up. He kept to his words, he never touched my body, he never kissed me, he never cuddled me, and he stood by his promises to my family and me. For example: there was a day when the day was getting dark, and all of a sudden there was a power cut   . There were other people in the living room   with   us   ; the power cut unexpected, and everywhere became dark. He held my hand and quickly walked me outside with him, then walked me home. These are life experiences that can be applied in courtship to preserve your   body from defilement. If you don't have parents, get an elder who can Godly channel you through, don't walk it alone.

Guard Your Thoughts:

You must understand that adultery often begins in the heart through what is known as the lustful thoughts and emotional dysfunctions leading to affairs and what is needed during that time is to occupy your thoughts with Biblical words, innovative activities and guard your imagination and heart by praying and seeking God's help to detest sin and meditate on your righteousness. You must fully understand that lustful thoughts are regarded as sin.

- Matthew 5:28, KJV

Imagine how you will feel   if another man or woman sees your nakedness that is meant only for your spouse if you are married, or when you are married. It is very disrespectful.

A lady said to me one day, Oh, Rev Janet, is it because you are a shy person? No, that is not the case   ; it has nothing to do with shyness. It has more to do with having integrity and respect for our God.

"It is God's will that you should be sanctified: that you should avoid sexual immorality; that each of you should learn to control your own body in a way that is holy and honorable". This teaches everyone that avoiding sexual sin and controlling your body with holiness is God's desire for all believers.

-1 Thessalonians 4:3-4, NIV

CHAPTER THREE

What does the Bible say about sharing your body outside your marriage?

Each time you commit adultery, you take away God's glory in your life. You reduce the connection between you and God. Your body is a temple of God   . This means that a believer's body is a temple of the Holy Spirit, so sexual sins like adultery are not just actions but actions against one's own spiritual identity and a compromise of your sacred body. You are not your own; you were bought at a price, and you must always remember this. God owns your body. It will shape you as a believer and remind you that you belong to God, having been purchased through Christ's sacrifice, and thus you must live in a way that honors your owner (GOD).

It is an ultimate call to use and respect the body that God has given you as a means to glorify God, reflecting on it daily that it is a living, sacred purpose, and the Spirit dwelling within it must be preserved.

The spiritual significance of our living

When it comes to the spiritual significance of our living, it shapes our understanding that engaging in adultery, and defilement of the body is seen as a spiritual act that entangles you with forces contrary to the spirit of God and your Godly spiritual nature and surrendering control to things not of God. I have listened to many people during counseling saying:

I can't control my emotions and feelings, or I am lonely, or I just can't keep my body for one person, I need to explore………..

Well, I have good news for you, if I can stay with a man for almost 23 years without defiling my matrimonial bed   or polluting my body, then you can do that also. Whatever God says to one, he says to all.

What I say to you, I say to everyone.

- Mark 13:37, NIV

You need the spirit of God to help you, and also have a mind   set of keeping your body as a temple of God.

In other words, the sexual intimacy shared between a man and woman is to be reserved for that couple alone.

Maybe you are thinking I can't control myself. Listen, God can control you, cast your burden unto God, and he will give you rest. When you surrender to God, God will take over your battles of sexual lust   .

Seeking Spiritual Counsel

I have shared with you many   real-life stories of how the spirit of fornication or adultery were speaking volumes in many people's lives, and the spirit were speaking through them that they can't leave, as these words were manifesting through them and declaring:

…… *I have emotions, I can't stay with one spouse,* etc.

Don't be afraid to seek counsel from marriage counsellors who can provide support and hold you accountable in your commitment to purity.

Listen to me, beloved   . I say this to you BOLDL Y: If my spouse can meet me as a virgin and I stayed

*faithful   to him for almost 23 years of togetherness
without defiling my body, you can do this as well.*

Prayer:

**I pray for you today that God will empower you
and make you stay faithful in your matrimonial
home in Jesus Name.**

CHAPTER FOUR

Married Couples: How do you stay faithful in your marriage?

Stay Relevant in your Home

To stay relevant in your home requires faithfulness in your marriage. It involves consistent Godly effort to prioritize your relationship with your spouse, maintain open and honest communication, and nurture your emotional and physical intimacy with your spouse.

Prioritize Quality Time with your Spouse

You must prioritize quality time with your spouse for couple's activities, or meaningful conversations to strengthen your bond and keep the connection fresh and shining. Make sure your children do not come in between those quality times; therefore, have an effective time planning for this quality time.

Praying Together in   Your Marriage

Praying together as a married couple is very essential in your marriage, it stems as a practice that fosters deep spiritual and emotional intimacy, it strengthens unity, improves effective communication, and provides protection against life's challenges. A husband and wife   who pray together, stay together, and have a peaceful   and loving home, including spiritual unity.

Two are better than one, because they have a good return for their labor~

- Ecclesiastes 4:9, NIV

Emotional Intimacy Should Never Be Compromised Between Couples

This can be achieved by focusing on active listening, empathy, and understanding your partner's emotional needs and building a deep emotional connection with one another. This is vital because it is fundamental to a secured, fulfilling, and lasting home. It produces freedom from fear, respect for each other's individual needs, and fosters growth and a stronger bond through genuine vulnerability and shared experiences.

The Bible says:

So they are no longer two, but one flesh. Therefore, what God has joined together, let no one separate.

- Matthew 19:6, NIV

Why is Emotional Intimacy Vital in Marriages?

It Fosters Connection and Support:

Couples who process a strong emotional bond provide themselves with comfort, respect, honour, refuge, and unwavering mutual support; this allows couples to grow together in one accord, understand each other fully, and navigate life's challenges together as a united team.

"Likewise, husbands, live with your wives in an understanding way, showing honor to the woman as the weaker vessel, since they are heirs with you of the grace of life, so that your prayers may not be hindered."

- 1 Peter 3:7, ESV

Love Solidifies the Foundation of Security and Trust

Having a strong emotional intimacy creates a safe space for both partners, allowing them to be their authentic selves, professing their LOVE as the foundation of all, without fear of judgment and criticism . This leads to a profound sense of security and trust in the relationship.

"And above all these things put on charity, which is the bond of perfectness."

- Colossians 3:14, KJV

This verse identifies love as the supreme virtue that unites all other qualities and strengthens the bonds within a marriage.

Critical for Longevity of Life, Divine Health & Health & Vitality

In a marriage that has no core emotional connection, such a marriage can feel incomplete, leading to feelings of trouble , loneliness, separation, distance, and helplessness . This can ultimately lead to the relationship failing in the short or long term. This can breed depression, regret, isolation, emotional disorder, and mental, physical, and social health issues. When the emotional connection is present and intimacy is not compromised, this gives longevity of life, divine strength, and health and vitality . In a case where the emotional connection is in decline due to age, staying very close, playful, and effective communication helps.

Having Quality Physical Intimacy in your Marriage is very Important

As couples, you must ensure that the quality of your physical intimacy remains very vibrant and must at all times be made a vital part of your relationship to foster closeness, a healthy marriage, a healthy life, and a peaceful home, free from insecurity, emotional neglect, and creating mutual respect for each party.

"Each man should have sexual relations with his own wife, and each woman with her own husband. The husband should fulfill his marital duty to his wife, and likewise the wife to her husband......

Do not deprive each other except perhaps by mutual consent and for a time, so that you may devote yourselves to prayer. Then come together again so that Satan will not tempt you because of your lack of self-control."

- 1 Corinthians 7:2-5, NIV

These Bible verses define sexual intimacy as a regular and mutual obligation within marriage, serving to strengthen the bond and prevent temptation.

Cultivate the Habit of Showing Appreciation to One Another

The attitude of expressing your love and appreciation for your spouse through words, actions, and kindness serves as a reminder to your spouse how much they mean to you. It displays respect and acknowledgement that you can feel their presence. Exercising this habit during intimacy and when not intimate is crucial for sustaining your marriage.

I have heard stories such as: *my husband just comes to me and asks to lay with him and goes straight to intimacy, and during intimacy he never talks to me, and once he is done, he just sleeps off.*

To every couple reading this, this is absolutely torture for any woman to experience. In every marriage, you must understand that there is a need for foreplay, as it increases the blood flow, lubrication, and emotional connection, which are crucial for comfort during intimacy. This reduces wounding and injuring your wife during intimacy.

Additionally, the experience shared by women during intimacy where there was no communication by their husband, and there was no emotional preparation for them by their husband, does not give liberty to the wife to deny her husband intimacy. What is needed during such a situation is effective open communication to address the issue.

What does the Bible say   on this:

1 Corinthians 7:3-5 teaches that God has intended sexual activity to be a regular and enjoyable thing for married couples, not a torture.

The husband must fulfill his duty to his wife, and likewise also the wife to her husband. The wife does not have authority over her own body, but the husband does; and likewise also the husband does not have authority over his own body, but the wife does. You can't deprive one another, except by agreement for a time, so that you may devote yourselves to prayer, and come together again so that Satan will not tempt you because of your lack of self-control.

- 1 Corinthians 7:3-5, KJV

CHAPTER FIVE

Now that you understand what the Bible says on intimacy in marriage, what do you do to enhance foreplay before intimacy?

Real Life Story

There was a newly wedded couple living in a neighborhood, every night we heard the wife screaming very, very loudly. Everyone thought the husband was physically abusing her (beating her). Until one afternoon, when the husband approached us and said he was having issues in his marriage . Any time he wants to be intimate with his wife, she is always screaming, and therefore, he has to stop. This is the rationale behind not having any children. The husband was asked how the screaming started during their intimacy, and when he described the situation. It was a really big trauma for the wife. There was no foreplay that could enhance emotional connection, and therefore, the wife's body was not ready, and sexual penetration into the vagina by the husband became a foreign object, forcefully gaining entrance into his wife's body. It was a seriously traumatic experience for her. Love making without foreplay can be a very daunting and traumatic experience for women in marriage.

The wife was invited to the next counselling session, and she had an open, honest communication during the session . She reported that she was planning to escape the marriage because she was in pain. The couple had effective person-centered therapeutic marriage counselling, and fore play teachings were explored for discussion, allowing the couple to discover their love gestures and romantic language that can prepare the wife for intimacy without torture. What they discovered to be their emotional connection was very simple, and this was showering together at night. You must understand that their method of foreplay, which was showering together at night, may look simple, but it saved their marriage. Showering together at night is a practice that can enhance intimacy and bonding for couples, but you must note that this is a personal choice for the couple, not a requirement for every couple's foreplay for emotional connection. Foreplays in marriages are meant to develop emotional connection and make intimacy a good experience and they are person-centered . This means every couple's love gestures are different, and it must be discovered by the couple themselves, with no interference from third parties. It is their personal choice, love code, and emotional connection dialing tones for a successful, joyful, and pleasurable intimacy experience.

This is a practical example of the wisdom of God at work. That home was almost destroyed, barrenness was added to their sorrow, not because they were not fruitful, but their intimacy was traumatic.

Prayer

I pray for every couple having marital breakdown, in the name of Jesus, the light of God will shine in your darkness, and you will enjoy your marriage as from today in Jesus Name.

Be Romantic

Foreplay is about being romantic with your spouse, and do you know what? Every little thing counts here . What do I mean by this? You must understand each other's romantic language. Romantic language could be small but thoroughly thoughtful gestures that symbolize your love. This could be tickling each other's ear or cheek, giving love notes, cooking a romantic dinner, presenting flowers, or wrapped gifts for no other reason than to say "I love you." These are examples of romantic gestures/ behaviors in marriages that go a long way in building or rebuilding intimacy.

To enhance emotional intimacy for foreplay, don't be afraid to go outside of your comfort zone, as approved by both of you as a couple, exercise some creativity, and then stick with what works best for you both as a couple.

These are the words of Solomon to his bride ; this is an expression of love language, and remember this is an allegory for Christ's love for the Church, which is depicted as a pure, precious, and His beloved entity.

You have stolen my heart, my sister, my bride; you have stolen my heart with one glance of your eyes, with one jewel of your necklace. 10 How delightful is your love, my sister, my bride! How much more

pleasing is your love than wine, and the fragrance
of your perfume more than any spice! 11 Your lips
drop sweetness as the honeycomb, my bride; milk
and honey are under your tongue. The fragrance
of your garments is like the fragrance of Lebanon.

- Song of Solomon 4:   9-11, NIV

Additionally, as a wife, you must not torture your husband during intimacy   . I have heard numerous stories from husbands complaining that their wives most times do not engage with them during intimacy. This is not right   ; however, there may be more to this, such as underlying issues, including stress, depression, anxiety, body dysmorphic disorder, hormonal changes, or a lack of emotional connection. It can also stem from feelings of insecurity, lack of trust, past trauma, or a perception that the intimacy is not emotionally fulfilling or lacking satisfaction. In such cases, we also offer professional help using specific psychological tool measurement, the Diagnostic and Statistical Manual of Mental Disorders (DSM-5), to diagnose and offer person- centered treatment.

CHAPTER SIX

The Disadvantages of Not Understanding Your Spouse's Needs in   Your Marriage

There will be Emotional Disconnection in the Marriage

When there is a lack of emotional connection, it can make your spouse feel misunderstood and unsupported, leading to distress, frustration, and a growing sense of emotional distance and disconnection.

There will be Withdrawal of Love and Creation of Conflict

Lack of intimacy amongst couples will give birth to further and continual cracks in the relationship and potentially cause marital issues, a permanent loss of effective verbal and non-verbal communication, and a decline in the couple's emotional connection.

Unmet Needs will be Present

There will be evidence of dissatisfaction and meaningful communication will be difficult between the couple in their marriage and this can create nagging, depression, loneliness, and emotional abuse.

What Can You Do Instead of Compromise in a Non-Effective Emotional Connection Situation?

Focus on Mutual Understanding and Stay Away from Self-blaming:

In this situation, couples should disapprove and stay clear of self-blaming. Instead, as a couple, you must work through the issues arising in your marriage and focus on actively listening to your spouse with the goal of truly understanding each other's feelings and perspectives on any flagged-up issues that can be done better for effective intimacy.

Be Open to Communicate Vulnerabilities

Instead of withdrawing from intimacy, find the avenue of working together through emotional openness, and this can help you with your emotional connection. Maybe your spouse is not doing what you would like or what will make you feel good as a man or woman during intimacy, you can go through it with him/her and work it out behind closed doors. Learn to talk to each other during intimacy, ask your spouse questions, do you like it if I touch you this way? Effective communication during intimacy bridges gaps. You must always remember that you both have become one as ordained by God ; therefore, be open to vulnerability in each other's arms during intimacy.

Identify, Communicate, and Prioritize your Core Needs and Values

Discuss with your spouse what your needs are and what you value during intimacy. You must understand that intimacy is for both of you to enjoy and replenish the world. I have heard numerous couples saying in the counselling session: *Oh, she can't satisfy me, or he can't satisfy me.* Such words are brutal and not godly. What you must do is to communicate your needs with your spouse . Once your needs are understood by each other, it will become easier for both of you as a couple to meet each other's needs.

The goal is building sustainable solutions that are not just a middle ground but that fosters genuine satisfaction for couples' needs, promoting deep connection and preventing the relationship from becoming sour, stagnant, unproductive, and unfulfilling.

Moreover, not adhering to compromising your core values and fundamental needs is crucial, along with having honest and effective communication with your spouse, so that the establishment of boundaries can be maintained. I have heard many stories during couple counselling, such as:

My husband keeps demanding for anus intimacy……..

I strongly believe everyone wants to read more about this, whether it is designed by God to have anus intimacy with your spouse. I will explain something to you: The anus was designed by God to push out waste, and not succumb to vigorous thrusting. Cleanliness is vital to Godliness ; therefore, the kind of bacteria in the anus can be very dangerous to the vaginal (birth canal), which can cause life-threatening infection for the couple. You must consider that you have rectal tissue that is fragile, and along with having hemorrhoid, it could lead to several complications, such as thrombosed hemorrhoids. For all who possess Godly wisdom, the answer is clear, that you can't change God's design, His creation, and the purpose of H is creation. God created everything on earth for a purpose. I believe you can't wake up in the morning and use your child's potty to make a cup of tea to drink. Conversely, you can't use the cup you use for your tea to wash your toilet/ washroom.

Marriage is a Lifelong Commitment

It is high time everyone getting married understands that marriage is a lifetime commitment, and not a playing field where you can be tossing balls around. Marriage is never child's play. This is all the more reason you must be   spiritually mature, not just in age, to have a healthy and lifelong marriage. Marriage is not a cloth that you change daily, weekly, monthly, or yearly. It is a lifelong commitment that requires mutual love, understanding, and Godly wisdom. God must be the foundation and the rock of your home   ; otherwise, it will never withstand any life turbulence. This is the reason why there are couple and marriage books, counselling teams/ coaches, mental health professionals and couple and marriage conferences and seminars that will equip you with God's wisdom for this lifelong journey, because human wisdom will fail you who   lly and fatally.

"What God has joined together, let not man separate."

- Mark 10:9, NKJV

This verse, echoed by Jesus in the Gospel, underscores that a marriage is a divine union not to be easily broken by human intervention, and it is a lifelong commitment, therefore, building it on God's rock is the key.

Your faithfulness in your marriage should never be less than 100% and must be a continuous choice that requires your conscious mindset that nothing will ever make you compromise with your body. To eradicate this, you must totally avoid risky situations, never entertain flirty comments from anyone, or engage in anything that could erode trust or cross emotional lines. I have used this method for numerous couples, and many people have used it, and there are great testimonies. You must learn to accept your spouse for who they are, acknowledging their positive and negative traits, and if there is any negative trait, please address it with prayer. For example: as a husband, you must understand that your wife may not have the same body in comparison to when you met her, most especially after child bearing. Wives go through ante natal and post natal stages . As a husband, you must love your wife all through these stages ; couple intimacy may decline, so learn to compensate for the vacuum of your level of intimacy that both of you usually have prior to the ante natal and post natal stages. This can evolve, changing your style of intimacy, adjusting to a new style of intimacy and loving yourself as a couple all through.

Believers are encouraged to study and meditate on the Word of God to know God's truth for themselves, rather than relying on external opinions or human wisdom in their courtship and marriage. It doesn't work. Remember, the just shall live by faith ; you must live by faith at all times, allowing it to saturate your heart and mind to change your life from the inside out. Endeavour totally to align with God's Will by consistently applying God's principles   . As a couple, you must foster a character that aligns with God and leading that will make you experience the fulfillment of your greater destiny.

CHAPTER SEVEN

Your Courtship and Marriage Must Mirror God's Image

The Bible made us to understand that: After God created the Earth (World) and the animals, He said, (the spoken word) "Let Us make man in Our image, according to Our likeness; and let them rule over the fish of the sea and over the birds of the sky and over the cattle and over all the earth, and over every creeping thing that creeps on the earth." This account continues, "God created man in His own image, in the image of God He created him; male and female, He created them".

- Genesis 1:26-27, KJV

Now, God's first purpose for creating man and woman and joining them in marriage was to mirror His image on earth   ; we must understand this. Remembering these words and giving   your attention to these words, which is *mirror His image,* will guide your steps in your courtship and marriage.

This Hebrew word for "mirror" means to reflect God, to magnify, exalt, and glorify Him. Your marriage should reflect God's image to a world that desperately needs to see who He is. Because we're created in the image of God, people who wouldn't otherwise know what God is like should be able to look at us and get a glimpse. That is how your courtship and marriage should look like.

Conflict Resolution in Courtship and Marriage

Having conflict resolutions as a couple within yourself must be embraced. You must adhere to practicing active listening and giving yourselves full attention. Effective listening skills with an open mind will help enhance mutual respect, never be judgmental, and try to see things from both sides' point of view, for the creation of an understanding atmosphere for each other's feelings and needs.

A couple asked me one day, how do I convey my emotions with my spouse without having communication barriers that will cause more trouble in their marriage. My answer was, ALWAYS use the "I"   s   tatements. How do you do this? You must be able to frame your concerns with a starting letter of "I feel" rather than using words that will make your spouse feel worse   about themselves (accusing finger), such as "you always", "you don't", or "you never".

This automatically eradicates blame   and focuses your own emotions and experiences, facilitating empathetic opening of the conversation in a more productive way that will resolve your marital issues flagged up during that discussion. Moreover, adapting this technique will strategize your focus on the issue, and not   criticize one another.

Mutual Respect Must Be Maintained

As couples, you must avoid derogatory words, such as name-calling, personal attacks, offence, and bringing up past grievances. Address current issues and make your conversation focused and direct on that specific issue identified. I have heard couples saying during counselling that: *My husband is not taking care of me financially, therefore, I denied him intimacy*. This is not right. If you want to discuss financial issues, don't bring your marital obligations into such an aspect. I believe you are not selling yourself to your husband.   Avoid retaliation at all costs. You must understand that retaliation must be avoided in marriage   ; instead, develop yourself to focus on managing your initial emotional reactions rather than focusing on the pain and anger you develop, otherwise, it will produce immediate striking back. In marriage, revenge often amplifies negative feelings and can destroy trust and open communication.

CHAPTER EIGHT

How Did God Design Marriage?

To Have a Lifelong Unity and Partnership:

Jesus stated and established that a man must leave his parents to cleave to his wife, and they will become one flesh. This signifies becoming one, and it is a profound spiritual and physical unity that is meant to last as God has designed it.

- Genesis 2:24, KJV

A Unique and Monogamous Union As Designed By God

God designed marriage to be monogamy and not polygamy, which means marriage is to be a private affair for the couple and not a public affair, where no third party interferes when not invited. Except the couple is having marital challenges and they are in need of a third party, such as consenting to a marriage counsellor, or a spiritual leader for divine intervention on their pressing issues.

Husbands, love your wife; wives, love and submit to your husband

Husbands are to love their wives, just as Christ loves His church; wives are to love and submit to their husbands, just like the Church submits to Christ. These are distinct roles as designed by God.

- Ephesians 5:25, KJV

30 Bold Marriage Affirmation Declarations

1. My spouse and I are created in God's image as helpers of our destinies, and therefore we complete each other.

- Genesis 2:8

2. I am grateful to God for His love and blessings that my spouse brings into my life.

- Ezra 3:11

3. Our love is blessed by God and we will be a source of inspiration and positive example for those around us.

- 1 John 4:17

4. I believe to see the best in my spouse and great qualities that make our marriage extraordinary successful.

- 1 Corinthians 13:   4-7

5. God has ordained love that flows effortlessly between us, creating a strong and unbreakable bond.

- Colossians 3:14

6. God has given us a relationship built on trust, communication, and mutual respect.

- 1 Corinthians 13:4-7

7. I am blessed by God for a deep and fulfilling love towards my spouse.

- 1 Corinthians 16:14

8. Daily our love grows stronger, deeper, and more resilient to defeat of life.

- Philippians 1:9

9. Every challenges of life is destroyed today, we are super united and defeating the devil and its craftiness by the power in the name of Jesus.

- Ephesians 6:12

10. I have faith in God that all our communications will strengthen the foundation of our love.

- Ephesians 3:17

11. In our marriage, we shared common goals, dreams, and aspirations, for a God ordained great destiny, filled with joy and success.

- Jeremiah 29:11

12. Father, I thank you for your supernatural grace of your love that is compassionate,

understanding, and unwavering as the foundation of our home.

- 1 Thessalonians 5:16-18

13. Father, we honour you in our home for our love flourishes daily in your uniqueness of Grace and Favour.

- Ephesians 4:32

14. Our home is built on the rock of God and the foundation of His word for a prosperous successful marriage.

- Matthew 7:24-27

15. I renounce the spirit of fears and doubts in our marriage.

- 2 Timothy 1:7

16. Our marriage is embedded in God's love, joy, peace, abundance, grace, favour, happiness, and mercy.

- 2 Peter 1:2

17. God make us prioritize our quality time together, for your divine strengthening of our emotional connection and intimacy in our marriage.

- Ephesians 4:2-3

18. Your love is the emblem of our marriage, giving us a deeper level of understanding and emotional connection and quality intimacy.

- Ephesians 5:25

19. We are your chosen glowing generation, called to manifest your divine agenda, multiply the world through your ordained procreation.

- Genesis 1:28

20. I declare my commitment to nurturing and cherishing the love we share as a couple in our marriage.

- Colossians 3:14

21. The love of God in our lives solidifies our love for each other, and serves as our source of strength that empowers us to overcome every obstacles and challenges of life.

- 1 John 4:19

22. Our marriage is a symbol of God's love, kindness, grace, peace, patience, goodness, faithfulness, fruitfulness, gentleness, and self-control.

- Galatians 5:22-23

23. Our marriage is surrounded with abundance of supernatural blessings that will be overflowing in our home.

- 1 Thessalonians 3:12

24. Our home is a beacon of light, holiness that is illuminating our path to a blissful fulfilling life together.

- Matthew 5:14-16

25. Father, I am thankful in advance for every special blessing in our marriage for making our marriage unique in your greatness.

- Psalm 128:3

26. Our home is a citadel of God, where thanksgiving takes place daily to appreciate God's faithfulness and fruitfulness.

- Psalm 100:4-5

27. I declare my home to be fruitful to the end with longevity of life, divine strength and health & vitality.

- Psalm 92:14

28. Father, I ask for the grace to accept my spouse for who you created my spouse to be.

- Ephesians 4:2-3

29. I declare that our marriage is a blessing to our generation.

- Proverbs 18:22

30. Our home will be an example of a Godly home that other homes will emulate as it is built on the solid foundation of the Integrity of God's words.

- Matthew 7:24-27

CHAPTER NINE

Are You Born Again?

Why is this necessary in your courtship and marriage?

To be saved and redeemed is necessary in any Courtship and Marriage, as it serves as a rock of discipline that guides you as couples to have self-control, principles, and the Godly character that you require to be equipped with, as this helps as Godly wisdom to build a healthy courtship and marriage. Without Godly wisdom (Heavenly wisdom) in your courtship and marriage, there will be difficulty in discerning a life partner that possesses similar spiritual values as you do, developing personal maturity, and establishing boundaries. A Godly courtship and marriage needs Heavenly wisdom to succeed and it requires making the word of God your priority daily and this aids your consistently applying principles of mutual respect, faithfulness, and shared responsibility, while also engaging in open communication and problem-solving to navigate life's challenges together. Remember, Heaven and earth will pass away, but none of the word of God will pass away, it eternally stands.

"Heaven and earth will pass away, but my words will never pass away."

- Matthew 24:35, NIV

To everyone reading this book today and that will love to give his/her life to Christ, or you were born again before but something happened and you are not saved anymore, pray this prayer out loud with me from the depths of your heart:

Salvation & Redemption Prayer

"Lord Jesus, I surrender my life to you today. Forgive me my sins; wash me with your blood. I believe you died for me, on the third day you rose again, that I may be justified. Right now, I believe that my sins are forgiven; I'm justified by your blood; I'm born-again; I'm saved; I'm a child of God; I'm free from the power of sin to serve the living God.

Prayer

Thank you, Jesus, for receiving me; thank you, Jesus, for restoring me; thank you, Jesus, for saving me.

Father, in the name of Jesus and by the Holy Spirit, empower my decision to pursue the advancement of your kingdom tirelessly to the end~ **Acts 1:8, KJV**.

I will make heaven in Jesus' name. Amen! !! !!!

CONGRATULATIONS! !! !!!

Now, I want you to decree to your courtship, marriage, and home, according to the word of God~

THIS AFFIRMATION BIBLE VERSE DECLARATIONS: NUMBERS 6: 24-27, NIV

REMEMBER YOU ARE WHAT YOU DECLARE WITH YOUR MOUTH: THE WORLD WAS FORMED WITH THE SPOKEN WORD OF GOD: THE BIBLE SAYS~ AND GOD SAID:

LET THERE BE LIGHT & THERE WAS LIGHT.

- GENESIS 1:3, KJV

I WANT YOU TO DECLARE   THESE WORDS TO YOURSELF DAILY:

24 *The Lord bless me*

   and keep me;

25   *The Lord make his face shine on me*

   and be gracious to me;

26   *The Lord turn his face toward me*

   and give me peace.

27 *"So they will put my name on the Israelites, and I will bless them."*

- Numbers 6: 24 -27, NIV

CONGRATULATIONS! !! !!!

1. *In the beginning was the Word, and the Word was with God, and the Word was God.*
2. *The same was in the beginning with God.*
3. *All things were made by him; and without him was not any thing made that was made.*
4. *In him was life, and the life was the light of men.*
5. *And the light shineth in darkness; and the darkness comprehended it not.*

- John 1:   1-5, KJV

Prayer

I decree in every courtship, marriage and homes, the LIGHT OF GOD will shine on you all and every darkness is shattered in Jesus Name. Amen!

ABOUT THE AUTHOR

Janet Adenusi is an Oracle of God and a vibrant, unique individual with a great personality, whom God has used to wipe many tears in this generation. A multi-book author. She is also a Medical Practitioner, a Leader in the Health Care Profession in the field of mental health, public health, and is involved in world health epidemiology interventions. Janet is a professor in the field of mental health, psychology, pharmacology, addiction, marriage, family and general counselling. Over the years, God has used her around the globe for greater and mighty Impacts, Deliverance, and Testimonies. She is the pioneer of numerous ministries, many Community Outreaches, public health projects, and foundations. Her media ministry stems from almost 2 decades and broadcasts through multi-media channels, with miraculous testimony galore from the media ministry and on the Covenant Breakthrough/ Liberation Hour Conference Meetings: Services are in- person, conference-telephone l   ine, and   Zoom. She has since enlarged the vision with great success on numerous community projects over the years, along with her better half, Kenny Adenusi, and they are blessed with six children.

THE BOOK

God is not a man that He should lie, nor a son of man, that He should repent. Has He said it, and will He not do it? Or has He spoken, and will He not make it good? - **Numbers 23:19, NKJV**

Whatever He says He will do, He will surely do it. When God showed me the gigantic cage of many people with shackles on their hands and legs. He commanded me to go into the world and speak to all; He has seen your afflictions, and heard your cry, He said He will Break Every Shackles in your relationships and marital lives. I speak loud to you, my Beloved, my Father in Heaven has come to your aid, you are free in   deed to have a God ordained, blessed courtship and marriage   . As you read this book, the promises of God for your life will be fulfilled in Jesus Name. According to the vision God showed me, this book has been written for you. I pray for your obedience, understanding, Godly wisdom, patience, strength, and knowledge. God   bless you.

Contact Details

Covenant Chapel Church Worldwide

Rev Kenny & Janet Adenusi: Visioneers

Email: Author Janet Team~

authorjanetteam@consultant.com
authorjanetteam@minister.com
authorjanetteam@secretary.net
authorjanetteam@gmail.com
authorjanetteam@post.com
authorjanetteam@mail.com

Facebook: Author Janet Team
Twitter: Author Janet Team
LinkedIn: Author Janet Team

www.ingramcontent.com/pod-product-compliance
Lightning Source LLC
Chambersburg PA
CBHW040826120726
48005CB00012B/1522